ART NOUVEAU

RESIDENTIAL MASTERPIECES 1892-1911

ARCHITECTURE

JUNICHI SHIMOMURA

Cadence Books San Francisco

First United States Edition, 1992
10 9 8 7 6 5 4 3 2 1

Executive Editor: Seiji Horibuchi
Managing Editor: Satoru Fujii
Translation: Matthew Thorn
Book Design: Shinji Horibuchi
Publisher: Masahiro Oga

Library of Congress Cataloging-in-Publication Data
Shimomura, Jun'ichi, 1952-
[Āru nūvō no meitei.   English]
Art nouveau architecture : residential masterpieces, 1892-1911 /
Junichi Shimomura. — 1st ed.
        p.   cm.
Translation of Āru nūvō no meitei.
ISBN 0-929279-82-4
1. Art nouveau (Architecture)   2. Architecture, Domestic.
3. Architecture, Modern—19th century.
4. Architecture, Modern—20th century. I. Title.
NA7125.S5513   1992
728".90"034—dc20   91-23220
                                                         CIP

Originally published in 1990 as *Art Nouveau Houses* by
Shogakukan, Inc., Tokyo, Japan

Art Direction and Design: Takanobu Morinaga and Dot Inc.

Cadence Books
A Division of Viz Communications, Inc.
P.O. Box 77010
San Francisco, California 94107

Printed in Japan

CONTENTS

Introduction

As the end of the twentieth century at last draws near, a sustained and intense interest in Art Nouveau seems to have firmly established itself. Emile Gallé, the Daum brothers, Louis Majorelle, and Alphonse Mucha—some of the craftsmen who represent this art—are again well known through exhibitions and the like. And yet, surprisingly few people seem to know that Art Nouveau was in fact a comprehensive art of urban spaces. I myself was unaware of this until I visited Europe for the first time in the spring of 1976. Because I was then studying art history, I decided to take a month to explore on foot the three cities of Paris, Florence, and Barcelona.

During my stay in Paris, the first example of Art Nouveau I encountered was an entrance to the *Métropolitain* train station. This work by Hector Guimard, which I had seen only in books, was near my pension. I had always thought you had to go to a museum to see such art, and I was astonished that Guimard's art appeared to be everywhere. Of course, the people coming and going didn't notice or stop to admire his creations. They just came out of the métro entrances and disappeared down the streets as normally as can be. With yellow subway tickets scattered about and the walls covered with posters and chewing gum, these architectural masterpieces melted into daily life.

It's amazing to think these masterpieces are still used today. The Parisians take all this for granted, but for me, who had never seen art as anything but art, it was quite a shock.

The same was true when I visited the Grands magasins du Printemps. I went up to the top floor to have lunch only to find that the ceiling was a huge dome of stained glass in floral patterns—its splendor and power of space vividly recalled the turn of the century belle époque. I could do nothing but gape at the colored light above me. When I recovered from my tourist's fascination and returned to my senses, I looked around and saw that the other people were calmly enjoying a chat as they ate their lunches or sipped their coffee.

Likewise, the Güell park in Barcelona is a perfect playground for children. When the neighboring primary school has recess, the children rush in. They run around the park, noisy and jostling. A group of boys amuse themselves with a game of soccer. The ball strikes relentlessly against the renowned dragon fountain and the stylized natural stone colonnades.

I'm certain I'm the only person who thought "ah, Gaudí!" and watched the children's games with a worried expression. During my repeated travels, my feet, as if of their own accord, took me to the Art Nouveau buildings that still remain in various cities and towns. It wasn't so much that I was attracted to the forms as I felt a strong desire to be immersed in spaces that were integrated with art. In Vienna, for example, Otto Wagner's Postal Savings Bank Office, which was completed in 1906, still functions as a main office for buying stamps, handing over account books, and exchanging money. Without a second thought, anyone can use the counters, writing desks, chairs, ashtrays, and wastepaper baskets carefully designed by Wagner. In Japan, certainly, such objects are kept in glass cases in museums. I quickly realized that Art Nouveau was concerned with creating buildings and facilities that supported everyday urban life. And anyone can plainly see that most of these buildings continue to be profoundly connected to daily life. In a sense, Art Nouveau is the art that made the modern city. In distant Japan, it's difficult to understand this fact.

Art Nouveau architecture may also be called the first popular or public art to come into prominence in the streets of Europe. Guimard's station has the same elegance as that of the benches and trees that sentimentally color the streets of Paris. In other words, Art Nouveau architecture was the outdoor furnishings of a hundred years ago. To be sure, the architecture of earlier periods—the churches, government buildings, and palaces—also served an important role in defining city structure. Often plazas and fountains were designed for public streets. Yet there is a strong sense that these structures were made to demonstrate to the people the authority and power of religion or politics. They were not simply facilities created for use in the daily lives of the citizenry.

With the coming of the age of Art Nouveau, however, architects began to design public facilities such as train stations, schools, and hospitals, as well as commercial ones—theaters, restaurants, cafés, and department stores. Moreover, they designed the houses and apartment buildings that form the basis of urban life.

For this variety of structures to appear in the city, dressed in the finery of Art Nouveau, the society that required them had to have formed. Late nineteenth-century Europe had undergone the industrial revolution. As a result, its urban population had increased drastically, and cities were pressed to make corresponding adjustments. Public gas, electricity, and sewage systems became widespread. Through the widening of main roads and the construction of railroad networks, cities began to take on their present appearances.

In terms of changes in people's lives, what stands out, after all, is the rise of a middle class that had gained power through industry and was replacing the former ruling class. As if to match the expansion of the city, the middle class began building mansions in the suburbs, returning to the towns to seek amusement and to shop. The development of Regent Street, London's famous shopping district, attests to these changes. In short, it was the age in which the prototype of urban consumer society as we know it today was being formed. Art Nouveau can be said to have designed the stage for this new life-style.

For example, most of Barcelona's Art Nouveau *modernismo* architecture is located in an area where the streets are laid out in a grid pattern. This more recently developed area was based on plans drawn up in the mid-nineteenth century. You look around the expansive intersections and on every corner stand beautifully colored towers or buildings fitted with stained glass bay windows. These charming expressions of *modernismo* give the town its grace and have become Barcelona's distinctive landmarks. Gaudí's Church of the Sagrada Familia and Casa Batlló speak to that fact, vividly.

Nearly one hundred years have passed since all these structures were completed. Most public facilities have had the benefit of preservation and restoration, but when it comes to commercial facilities, the reality is that most have been lost to us. The Innovation department store in Brussels, designed by Victor Horta, has long since burned to the ground. The greater part of Charles Rennie Mackintosh's Tearooms in Glasgow has also been lost, and no one will ever be able to enjoy a cup of tea there again.

Even more severe than the disastrous state of commercial institutions is the loss of private residences. Among the newly risen middle class that supported the prosperity of Art Nouveau residences, many managed to build their fortunes in a single generation. Few families, however, were able to maintain their wealth over several generations, and as a result, some homes have fallen into ruin and decay. Interiors were also often redecorated to reflect changing tastes. It's not difficult to imagine Art Nouveau, considered an old-fashioned style in the twenties and thirties when Modernism and Art Deco were popular, disappearing from homes bit by bit.

Just as Art Nouveau buildings were the first urban designs accessible to the populace, so were Art Nouveau homes the first in which the new twentieth-century urban life-style was conducted. Although I use the term populace, the families who lived in such houses were barely a handful. All of the residences presented in this volume are truly mansions, startlingly spacious and furnished with numerous rooms. Even so, their owners often would dress up and head for a restaurant or concert hall. On weekends they invited guests and threw house parties. Visitors and hosts would while away sunny afternoons, reclining on sofas in the bay windows. Many facets of the life-style these people developed in their Art Nouveau mansions are linked to the sensibilities of contemporary life.

Fortunately, several residences survive in Europe in which the interiors remain just as they were originally designed. They can be called without exaggeration a precious cultural inheritance of the twentieth century. To leave a record of the few but beautiful interiors and to ponder the life-style of the people who built the foundation of our own life-style—these were the ideas behind my desire to bring together the present volume.

The photographs shown here were taken over seven years beginning in the spring of 1983. I photographed each of the three houses examined in detail, Casa Batlló, Maison Horta, and Hill House, on several occasions because they are rare works that convey the essence of Art Nouveau residential interiors. As a result, differences of season and time occur throughout the photographs. Forgive this point—it stems from my desire to create a more precise record.

In the realization of this volume, I received the cooperation of many people. I would like to express my gratitude with all my heart for their kindness.

I have tried to offer a commentary on each house as if the reader and I were visitors to that house, with the hope that this will aid the reader as he or she "walks" through the photographs.

April 1990

Chapter 1

CASA BATLLÓ

1 9 0 4 - 1 9 0 6

Antonio Gaudí

Barcelona, Spain

1

1
The exterior of Casa Batlló, seen from
the Paseo de Gracia, as the morning
sun skims the roof.

2 Chimneys cluster on the roof, their tops capped with triangular hats and their trunks covered in glass mosaic.

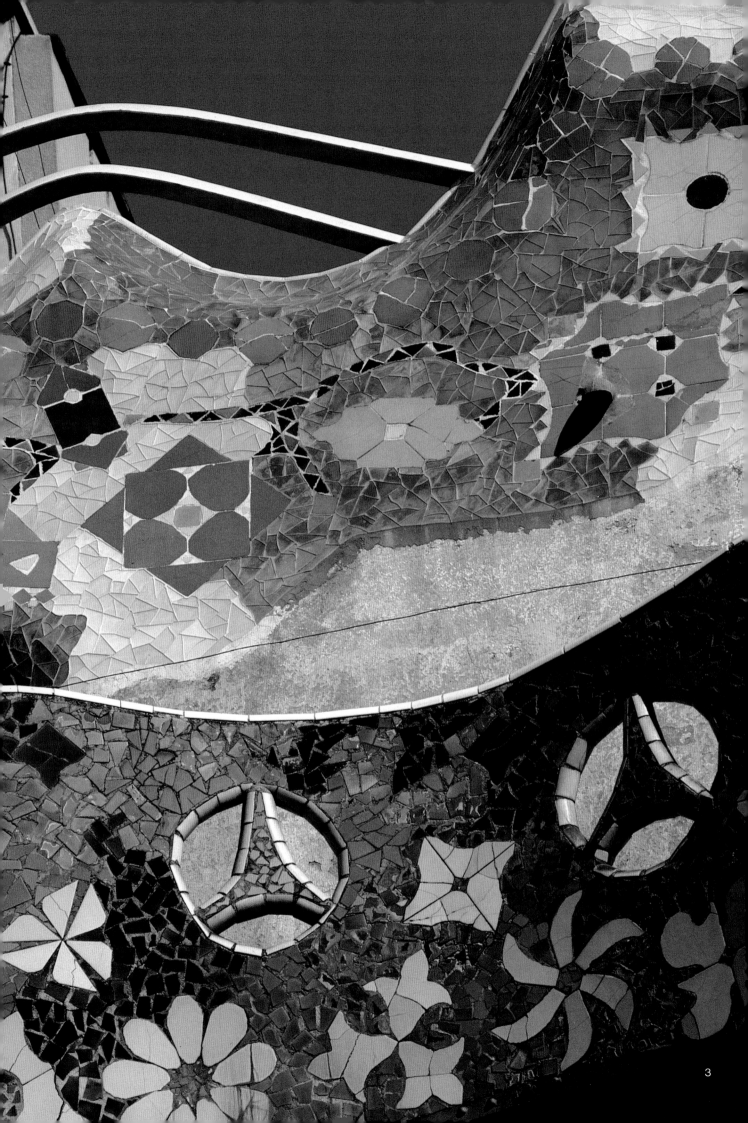

4

The mosaic patterns that cover the
periphery of the roof facing the rear
garden were designed by Gaudí's
apprentice, Jujol.

4
The crest of the roof and the tower. The
cross decorating the tower is characteristic
of Gaudí's design.

5　The wall of the rooftop is irregular, like the ridge of a mountain without a single level surface.

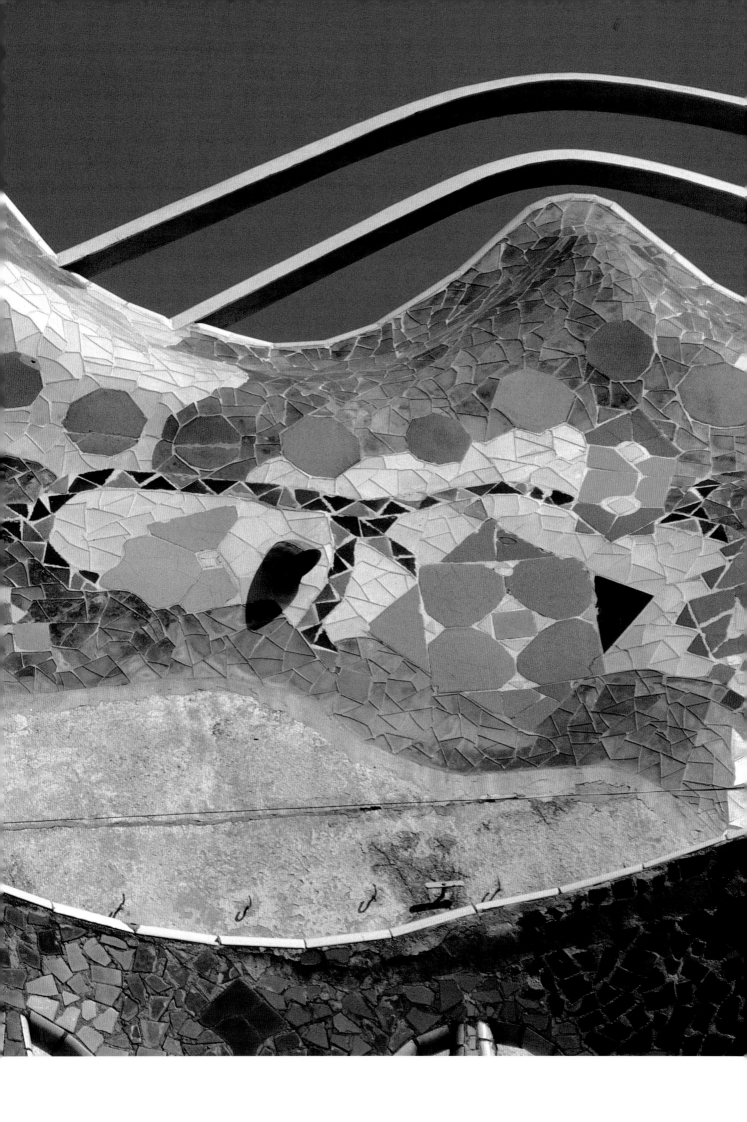

6
An observation window in the roof overlooking the Church of the Sagrada Familia.

7
An overall view of the roof with the
stairwell skylight in the foreground.

8

8
The roof tiles in various colors. The
gold letters symbolize the holy family.

9
One of the wrought iron balconies
designed by Jujol, with spiral trimming.

10
The undulating front wall is said to
represent the Mediterranean.

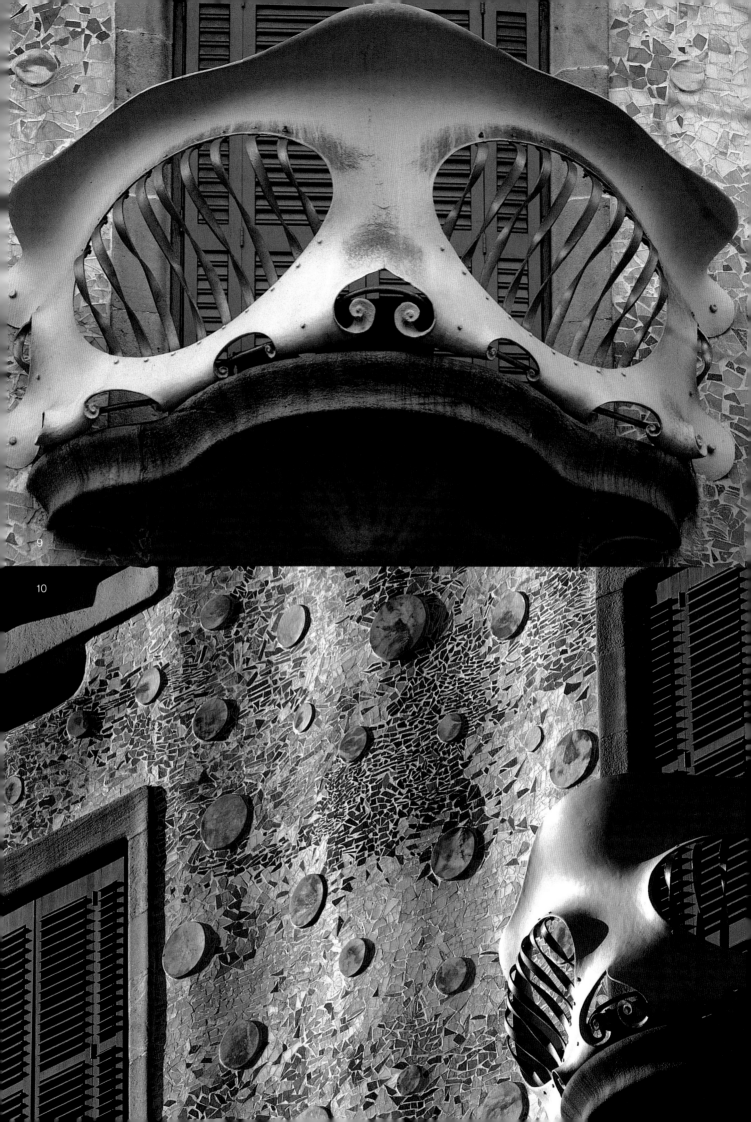

11
The bay window of the Batlló family
salon. The wave pattern of the window
matches the undulations of the wall.

12
The sandstone entrance to the first floor.
A perfect form by Gaudí, who was well
versed in the handling of stone.

13
The finish of the plaster wall of the entrance hall achieves the effect of a mosaic through color and line.

14
The porter's lodge at the entrance to the Batlló family home. The slight depression in the wall creates an intimate atmosphere.

15
The T-shaped steel post, shaped into a dragon, was an innovative support structure for the stairwell.

17

16
A skylight in the science fiction–like roof
of the porter's lodge diffuses the light.

17
The common staircase continues the
smooth flow from the entrance hall.

18
From below, the stairwell, which serves as
a patio, resembles light pouring into a cave.

19
A terrace opening onto the stairwell.
Even the metal network of the parapet
has a voluptuous look.

20
The interior of the top floor, with its
skylight, has a high-tech flavor.

21
The shape of the steps demonstrates
the attention Gaudí paid to the way
people move.

22
The door to one apartment. The flesh-
like parquet work is scattered with roses.

23
The transition of colors in the tiles was
designed to maintain light evenly from
floor to floor.

22   23

24
When the staircase to the Batlló home
completes a 180-degree turn from the entrance, a skylight peeks around the corner.

25
The upstairs hall window facing the patio.
The shape is irregular, but the opening
mechanism is sound.

26
Skylights in the wall facing Casa Amatller
bring light to the upstairs.

27
From above, the walls surrounding the
wooden staircase look like the inside of
a conch shell.

28
An overall view of the upstairs hall. The
handrail of the stairs and the parapet
join to form a single spiral.

29

29
The waiting room door that leads to the
office; a display case with mirrored
glass also serves as a full-length mirror.

30
The intimate waiting area with its fireplace gently welcomes visitors.

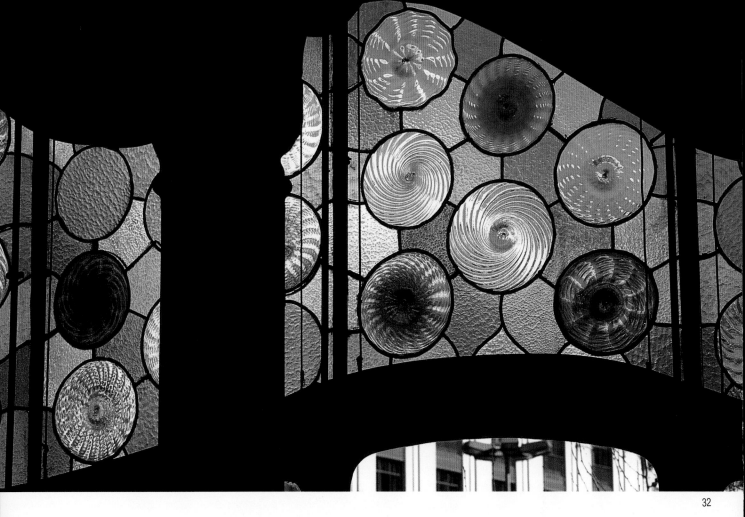

32

31
An overall view of the waiting room. The small space is rich in variations.

32
Spirals of different sizes were used in the colored glass covering the upper portion of the salon windows.

33
Movable folding doors separate the salon and office.

34 The ceiling was shaped into a huge whirlpool by applying plaster to a grid hurdle fixed to the ceiling.

35
In an upper corner of the salon, the doors bulge slightly, continuing the rounded shape of the wall.

36
The decorated divider at the top of the door shines in the light of the waiting room lamps.

37 38

39

37
The brass handle is tipped with a spiral,
forming an easy-to-grip curve.

38
Vents on either side of the door lead to
neighboring rooms. The covers resemble the spine of a dragon.

39
The handle for raising the window
matches the doorknobs on the apartment doors.

40

41

40
An overall view of the salon as seen from the office. The area left of the pillars was added to form the bay window.

41
The spirals carved into the sandstone pillars that support the bay window alcove augment the feeling of strength.

42
The salon with its huge windows faces the sunlight. One window is half open.

43
A round wooden vent designed to open and close by rotating its interior spiral cutouts.

44

44
The bars in front of the bay window,
decorated with flowers, may symbolize
the bones of a dead dragon.

Gaudí: Beyond Tradition

Barcelona, the second largest city in Spain, overlooking the Mediterranean to the east and gently sloping toward Mount Tibidabo in the west, has two faces, one old and one new: the Gothic district with Barcelona Cathedral in the center of an intricate network of narrow roads and the surrounding urban area with its streets set in a regular grid pattern.

The new city area, which comprises the largest part of Barcelona today, developed during the expansion begun in the late nineteenth century. With an infusion of capital from local textile and steel industries creating the economic groundwork for expansion, a fever of development swept the outskirts of the old Gothic district. At the same time, the storm of Art Nouveau was raging in Europe. Art Nouveau architecture soon appeared in Barcelona, which, although a Spanish city, was keenly interested in Parisian trends in art and ideas. The architecture of *modernismo*, the Spanish version of Art Nouveau, sprang up here and there, shaping the new city area. Antonio Gaudí's representative work, the Expiatory Church of the Sagrada Familia, is in this section of Barcelona.

Antonio Gaudí, the quintessential *modernismo* architect, was born in 1852 in Reus, a town near Barcelona. For generations, his forefathers were metalworkers producing pots and pans. It's conceivable that the tremendous amount of grave yet fluid ironwork adorning his buildings was a result of his family's trade. From 1872 to 1877, Gaudí studied at the School of Architecture of the University of Barcelona. Since he was not blessed financially and had lost one family member after another, Gaudí was forced to work part time at numerous architectural firms from the time he began as a student.

After acquiring his architectural license in 1878, Gaudí became productive on a grand scale. The work of his early period, starting with his first project, Casa Vicens (1888), and including such representative works as the Colegio de Santa Teresa de Jesus (1890) and the Villa Bell Esguard (1908), preserves a richness of historical styles rather than achieving anything that could be called Art Nouveau. In Catalonia, which embraces Barcelona as its capital, three architectural traditions—Romanesque, Islamic, and Gothic—coexist. Through his studies of structures and his investigations into the ornamentation of these three design traditions, Gaudí was groping toward an architecture for the new age. This study of old forms in search of new was a characteristic of *modernismo* that Gaudí shared with other architects.

It was not until the coming of the twentieth century that Gaudí began to develop the curiously shaped architecture with which we are so familiar. It seems that through his understanding of historical architectural structure, he was able to discover possibilities for new spatial forms. His new shapes may also have been the result of long, painstaking observations of nature. In the first two decades of the century, Gaudí built a church for Güell's workers' colony; Güell Park, famous for the undulating shapes of its benches; and two apartment buildings, Casa Batlló and Casa Mila. All of these works give the impression that they are about to move, a characteristic unusual for Art Nouveau in which designs tended to be planar from beginning to end.

In later years, Gaudí, having lost his longtime patron, Count Eusebio Güell, poured all his energy into the construction of

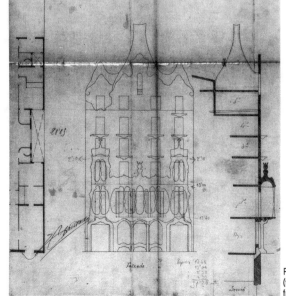

Plans submitted for approval of building (front and interior section), from the *Barcelona Historical Archives*

CASA BATLLÓ

the Church of the Sagrada Familia. Gaudí was a devout believer in Christ, and it is said that he adhered to the simple life-style of a monk in his own life. When the nativity facade, one of the church's entrances, was nearly 80 percent complete in 1926, he was hit by a streetcar and killed. The Church of the Sagrada Familia remains incomplete although construction continues to this day.

The Narrative Quality of Casa Batlló

The six-story apartment building Casa Batlló, which has undergone exterior restoration in recent years, faces onto the Paseo de Gracia (photo 1), the fashionable shopping street that extends from La Rambla Avenue in the old district of Barcelona. Next door is Puig's Casa Amatller and a few doors down is a building by Domènech—the works of the three great masters of *modernismo* are gathered in one block. Casa Batlló is Gaudí's renovation of a stone apartment building built during the city's expansion in 1877. It is named after its owner, the businessman Jose Batlló Casanovas.

At first sight, it is difficult to believe that Gaudí simply renovated the building. The bone-shaped stone frames that form the bay windows of the first and second floors, the mosaic of colored pieces of glass that covers the entire outer wall, the roofing tiles that change into seven colors — any and all of these demonstrate an extraordinary coherence and give the building sparkle (photos 8-12).

Gaudí's primary renovations are as follows. The outer wall was scraped away until only the window frames were left; an undulating pattern was then added with lime mortar and inlaid with colored glass (photo 10). Steel balconies with eerie coun-

tenances were placed on the windows. These cosmetic touches were added to erase the rather depressing appearance created by the building's northern exposure on its street side. The stone window frames of the first and second floors, the soaring tower, and the roof are also part of these main exterior renovations. For the interior, Gaudí redesigned the Batlló family residence, which occupies the first and second floors, the common stairwell used for the apartments, and the rooftop patio (photos 2-7). At present, the floors previously occupied by the Batlló family are owned by an insurance company, and the dining hall and many of the rooms have been altered. The only original Gaudí interiors are the stairwell and a few rooms, including the adjacent waiting room and salon. In these areas, however, spaces unfold that are uniquely the architect's and which emanate an appeal not found in any other Art Nouveau architecture.

What is being expressed by the strange shape of the exterior? With its stone window frames, columns that look like bones or legs, and scalelike tiles, the exterior is not simply eccentric, but it may even create a disturbing impression. What is surprising is that the client allowed his building to be transformed into so grotesque a shape.

It is generally assumed that the exterior motif reflects the story of Saint George, the patron saint of Catalonia, slaying the dragon, a tale that has been told by people for generations. It is said that the roof is the dragon's back and the window frames the dead creature's bones. The tower that reaches to the heavens (photo 4) is the lance, representing the saint's victory. If Gaudí's renovation retold a legend dear to the Catalonians, it is likely that his client, too, would have approved of the design. There is another more recent theory that the mushroom house in an

Layout of second floor

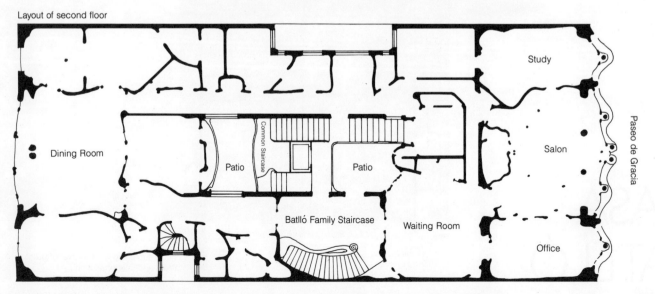

operatic version of *Hansel and Gretel* first performed in Barcelona in 1901 was the original inspiration for Casa Batlló. In either case, the unification of an exterior design around some kind of narrative is something found in no other contemporary architect.

Supporting the sandstone bay windows modeled after the dragon's bones, several columns extend upward from the ground. An entrance opens out from the left-most columns, which resemble the legs of an animal. The appearance is like that of a cave, and we feel an involuntary urge to enter. Though the entrance hall that leads inside is dim, the plaster walls curve gently, extending deep into the interior, and we feel as if we are being invited into a grotto or the belly of a huge animal (photos 13-16). Once inside, the hall separates into the staircase leading to the apartments and the private staircase of the Batlló family. The two are divided artfully by a rounded wall that gently directs our footsteps upward.

Light Filling Gentle Spaces

Without further delay, let us pay a visit to the Batlló home. The private wooden staircase continues upward. Then, surprisingly, it takes a one-hundred-and-eighty-degree turn, as if wanting to engulf the visitor. Accustomed to square staircases, we can only stare wide-eyed at the stairwell shaped like a conch shell (photos 24-28). When we reach the point where the staircase makes a broad curve, soft light falls from above, coming in through the skylight built into the ceiling. This light leads us through the darkness of the staircase, which rises gently and is easy to climb. They say that Gaudí climbed up and down the actual site over and over before deciding on the gradient.

Upstairs, the affixed wooden railing twists up into a tight spiral, a lamp poised at its tip (photo 28). Gaudí made use of the spiral motif throughout the interior design, from the large whirlpool of the staircase to the movement of the railing.

Our steps, having moved naturally through the cavelike, continuous space from the entrance hall to the stairs, stop momentarily at the upstairs hall (photo 25), facing out onto the patio, and the waiting room (photos 29-31), which was designed to be a front room to the salon. These rooms, too, are surrounded by curving, irregular walls. It is as if we were being gently enveloped, and a feeling of relief fills our heart. The sense of incongruity felt on first encountering this residence has already disappeared. The alcove in the waiting room is particularly outstanding (photos 30-31). Within this space, benches that seat two are positioned to the right and left of a central fireplace. The alcove walls are covered with fireproof tile, in a finish that contrasts with the plaster walls of the room. The space is so intimate that it is tempting to call it the refuge of the house.

Light comes softly through the spiderweb-shaped, stained glass dividers into the dim waiting room. When we open the doors, the salon, which faces the main street, opens out before us (photo 42). This salon, in which the sandstone window frames can be seen in silhouette, overlooks the city street like a whale with its huge mouth agape (photos 32-44). The spatial continuum which started at the entrance has become gradually darker until it is here suddenly set free in a burst of light.

The salon ceiling impresses us with yet another large whirlpool (photo 34), which seems to draw in the window-side pillars and the surrounding walls. A lamp hangs quietly at the central core of the whirlpool. We notice without surprise the colored glass (photo 32), engraved with spiral patterns, set into the upper portion of the bay window alcove (photo 40). The angle of the bay windows gives this space a curved, bulging effect. These windows slide up and down effortlessly through the use of weights. Gaudí's beautifully decorative designs also possess a definite functionality. The slightly curved, slim door handle is truly easy to grip (photo 37). For Art Nouveau artists, a doorknob was a perfect opportunity for decorative detail. Gaudí, however, limited himself to a small spiral drawn by the tip of the handle. The salon and adjacent office are separated by a movable wooden divider (photo 33)—Gaudí's innovative attempt at structurally eliminating internal walls in bonded buildings. He achieved an opening of interior space as early as the beginning of the twentieth century. The appeal of this salon lies foremost in a functionality that suggests a modern life-style. The ornamentation is relatively moderate, and the spirals, large and small, act in unison to create a modest interior. Comfort was Gaudí's first priority.

Unfortunately, most of the original furniture designed by Gaudí for the salon and the remodeled rear dining room have been lost. The ceiling lamps in the stairwell and the salon are also not his work. The originals were like chandeliers, surrounded by strings of glass beads.

In the communal apartment stairwell (photos 17-23), which also serves as a patio, we can see the fastidiousness with which Gaudí used light. The stairwell is lit by natural light from a skylight in the rooftop (photos 7 & 20), a skylight whose parabola-shaped steel frame is set with glass. The apartment building is six stories high so daylight does not reach ground level. Because of this, Gaudí varied the color of the tiles covering the wall in

order to moderate the contrasts in the light. The square tiles transform from pure white on the first floor to deep blue on the top floor. The size of the windows in the rooms facing onto the patio also vary, becoming smaller toward the top of the building (photo 23). Though our eyes tend to fix on its ornamental quality, Gaudí's interior design is almost always concerned with ease of use.

When we think of Art Nouveau, we usually think of sensual ornamentation with natural motifs of flowers, trees, and plants. Strangely enough, not a single such design can be found in Casa Batlló. This does not mean that there is no ornamentation. On the exterior there is quite a bit of decoration, including the colored glass mosaic of the front and the floral-patterned tile mosaic facing the rear garden (photo 3). Gaudí does not, however, attempt detailed representations of plants. Though he boldly uses a large dot pattern in the stained glass interior windows, as if he were constructing an abstract painting, he shows surprisingly little interest in detailing the forms.

Perhaps for Gaudí, interior design was first and foremost the construction of space. The transitions between rooms and staircases weave together freely in both fast and slow motion, and his expressive use of light makes those transitions visual. In short, the main theme of Casa Batlló is the functional continuity of space.

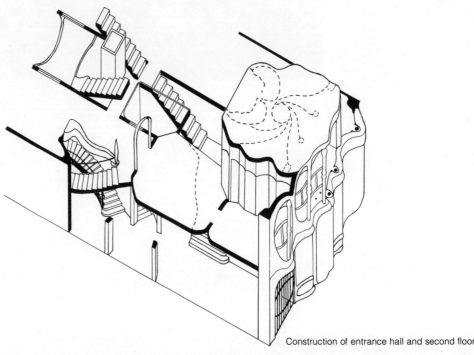

Construction of entrance hall and second floor

Chapter 2

MAISON HORTA

1 8 9 8 – 1 9 0 1

Victor Horta

Brussels, Belgium

45

Exterior view from rue Américaine. The
height and design of the studio are different from the main house.

46 The rear garden uses a geometric pattern found in many other Horta designs, such as the backs of his chairs.

47
The symmetrical guardrail on the terrace
of a garret room. The windows of the
study are below.

48
The frosted glass floor of the salon balcony overhangs the entrance.

49
The balcony is a bouquet of ironwork
held together with bolts.

48

49

50

50
Boot scrapers between the entrances to the house and the workshop.

51
The cast-iron crosspiece was designed primarily to coordinate with the stone.

52
The front door of the house. The metal fitting of the door chime hangs near the street number.

53
The handle of the front door, carved with several delicate lines, is cast in bronze.

54
Horta's name is cast in the top of the mail slot in the center of the studio door.

52

53   54

56

55
The symmetrical inner double door is
as colorful as the wings of a butterfly.

56
The entrance hall beyond the inner
doors. A soft light falls from the top of
the stairs.

57   58

57
An oak handrail begins its ascent from a marble pedestal in the entrance hall.

58
A supporting post in the entrance hall also serves as a heater. Heat-radiating brass plates encircle the central pipe.

59
Looking up the stairwell from the hallway. The edges of the ceiling have been trimmed with gold.

60
The second floor, a view of the stairwell and dining room from the music salon.

59

60

EN HOMMAGE A VICTOR HORTA
LA COMMUNE DE SAINT-GILLES A
SAUVE CETTE MAISON, OU VECUT ET
TRAVAILLA LE GRAND ARCHITECTE

62   63

61
An overall view of the dining room as
seen from the smoking room. Further
back, the salon windows open onto rue
Américaine.

62, 63
The ash-framed divider between the dining room and smoking room.

64
The railing of the steps divides the dining room and salon.

66

65
The railing extends up to form the arm
of the sofa in the music room.

66
The oak handrail of the spiral staircase
forms a corner like a tangled thread.

67 The railing, although composed from several sections, is as smooth as if carved from a single piece.

68
The door to the hidden service staircase
is also decorated with stained glass.

69
A ceiling lamp in the stairwell. The motif
resembles the form of a flower like a
violet.

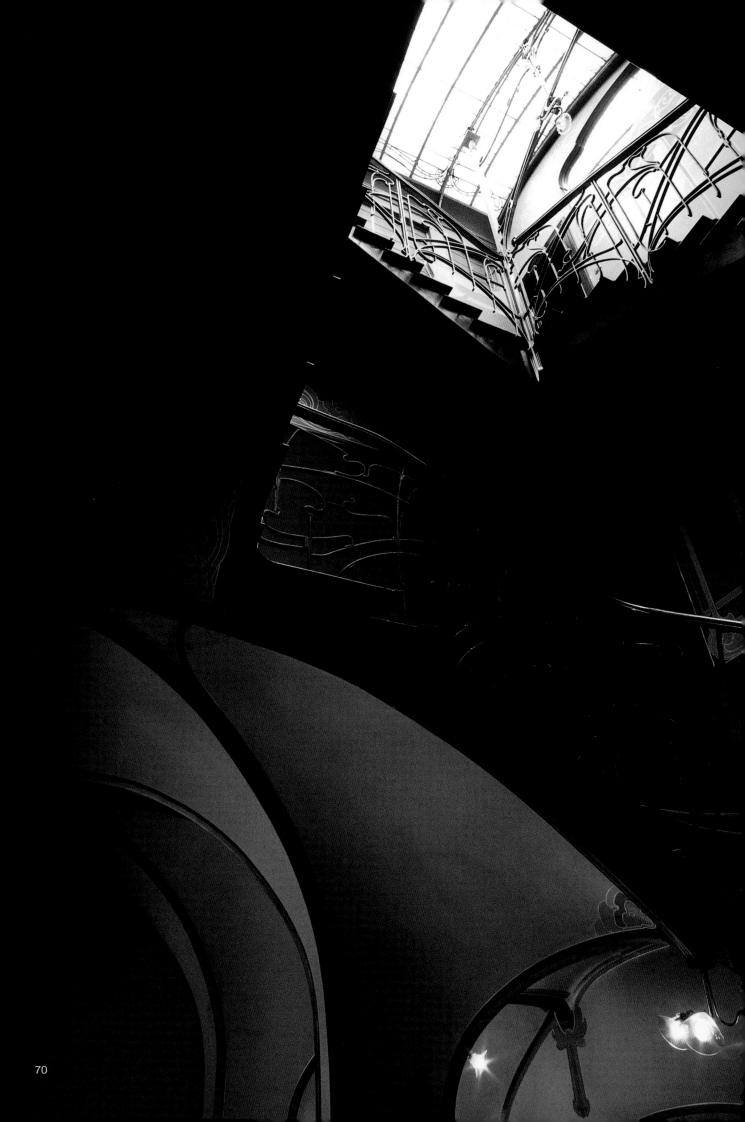

71

70
Viewed from below, the spiral stairwell
turns into a well of light.

71
Lamps in the stairwell twine around
each other like plants extending their
curling tendrils.

72
The glass-domed skylight which forms
the roof scatters the light.

73
The oil-painted brown background of the
walls transforms brightly as it rises
toward the ceiling.

74
On the top floor landing, mirrors on
either side extend the narrow space.

75
Brass decoration weaves intricate lines
around the posts which form the axes
from which the stairs hang.

76
On the oil-painted walls, floral patterns
are drawn in with varnish mixed with
gold dust.

77
The railing is formed of complex lines,
but its pattern is basically symmetrical.

78 Looking down the funnel-shaped stairwell to the white marble of the entrance hall.

79
A mirrored wardrobe is built into the
third floor dressing room.

80
The glass door separating the dressing
room from the third floor landing lets in
light from the hall.

81
The third floor study also serves as a
private living room. The wallpaper is a
willow pattern by William Morris.

82
The metalwork of the door handles
is one of the details to which Horta
directed his attention.

81

82

83
The simple ceiling of the study, so different from the interior of the second floor.

84, 85
One of the distinctive characteristics of Horta's chairs are the backs, which look like spread wings.

84

85

86
A daybed for napping. The wood is
American ash, Horta's favorite.

87, 88
Original Horta furniture, other than that
made for his home, is also on display
in the museum.

87   88

89
A writing table attached to the wall of the reception salon which extends into the studio side of the building.

90
A closet in the bedroom hides a urinal built into the bathroom behind the bedroom.

91
This screen for changing or bathing was not originally made for Horta's house.

93

92
An elaborate parquet service door that opens onto the dining room from the pantry.

93
The dining room lamps hang like bouquets from the ceiling. The edges of the shades are tinted red and green.

94
The handle of the pantry door is the most elaborately crafted handle in the Maison Horta.

94

95

95
Gold-painted iron reinforcements to the
arches support the dining room ceiling.

96
The lamps attached to the four corners
of the smoking room ceiling resemble
dried flowers.

97
The doors of the built-in display case in
the dining room are bordered with
elaborately carved wood.

96

98
Horta's friend Dubois designed the silver candelabra in the center of the dining table.

99
Horta designed even the hinges and keyholes of his furniture.

100
A heater occupies the lower portion of the display case. Public gas had already become common.

101
Sheet copper divides the marble mosaic border from the wood of the dining room floor.

102
The pillar that separates the dining
room and the music salon.

103
The stairs flow gracefully into the salon,
which overlooks rue Américaine.

104

The rear garden as seen through the
doors of the smoking room. The furniture was collected in later years.

Horta: The Man Who Lived Alongside Art Nouveau

The Belgian architect Victor Horta is considered one of those who lit the flame of the Art Nouveau movement in architecture and interior design. Horta's private home, which he built at the very end of the nineteenth century when he was at the peak of his career, is known as Maison Horta. In the nineteen-year period between its completion in 1901 until he sold it in 1919, he absorbed himself day and night in his designs at this urban residence, which included both a living area and a studio.

Today, the house is the property of the Saint Gilles district of Brussels and is open to the general public as the Musée Horta (Horta Museum). Rue Américaine, where the Horta home and studio are located, is about twenty or thirty minutes by streetcar from Grand-Place, the center of Brussels with its medieval city hall and guild house. A quiet street, rue Américaine is in one of the residential areas developed in Brussels toward the end of the nineteenth century.

Victor Horta was born in 1861 in the northwestern city of Ghent in Belgium. As a child he loved music and later went out of his way to fit the Maison Horta with a salon specifically designed for the appreciation of music. After studying architecture at the academy in Ghent, he worked under a Parisian interior decorator for a year and a half, starting in 1878. In 1884, he began working at the Brussels studio of Alphonse Balat, the Royal Architect to King Leopold II. Balat was constructing a huge palace greenhouse, working with cast iron and glass,

and it is said that during this time Horta awoke to the possibilities in curvaceous steel decoration for expressive details. While working under Balat, he received a Royal Committee Award and set off on a study tour of Paris and Cologne. In 1889, he visited the Paris World's Fair and witnessed large-scale steel-frame structures, such as the Eiffel Tower, that were then under rapid construction.

In 1893, Horta worked on Hôtel Tassel in Brussels, the private home of a university professor. This home was the first Art Nouveau residence in Europe and Horta's first prominent work. Its construction led to his overnight rise to the status of darling-of-the-day. He went on to work not only on other residences but also on a variety of public and commercial buildings, including Solvay House (1898), Van Eetvelde House (1900), Maison du Peuple (the People's House) (1897), and the Innovation department store (1903). Through these buildings Horta created an Art Nouveau sensation in the streets of Brussels.

In his later years until his death in 1947, Horta's activity declined along with the popularity of Art Nouveau. He confined himself to social activities such as serving as the president of the Fine Arts sector of the Royal Academy of Belgium (1925). In 1932, Horta received the title of Baron. In the Brussels Central Railway Station and several other works representative of his later years, we no longer see the gorgeous style characteristic of Art Nouveau.

Today, most of Horta's important works have been lost, and only a few small residences remain. Maison Horta is therefore a precious record. As a product of Horta's most creative period, it exhaustively preserves to this day the artistic style that sparked the flame of Art Nouveau.

MAISON HORTA

Front view of Maison Horta and the studio

101

Tranquil Atmosphere

Today, the rue Américaine is a residential street in the Saint Gilles district, with a few office buildings and restaurants mixed in. Just as most of the Art Nouveau architecture in Paris is found in outlying areas developed after the nineteenth century, the Saint Gilles district is one of those areas of Brussels established during its later expansion. Here, in 1898, Horta purchased a long and narrow lot, 130 feet deep and 40 feet wide.

Most of the surrounding houses, though made of stone, are elaborate in design while lacking ornamental columns, which indicates that the entire area was built in comparatively recent times. We can surmise that it was not until the twentieth century that the completion of streets with sidewalks was made: the front door of every house, beginning with the Horta house, has a boot scraper alongside it to clean off mud from the streets.

The exterior of Maison Horta is made of whitish sandstone, an extremely common material in the architecture of the day. In Maison du Peuple and the Innovation department store mentioned earlier, Horta achieved breakthroughs in exterior design through his extensive use of steel and glass. In his own home, you might expect even more novel experimentation. And yet, this exterior is the opposite in its restrained tranquility (photo 45). Its look is so subdued that the house seems to disappear among the neighboring homes, and anyone who did not know it was there might walk by without noticing it. Here we can see Horta's somewhat conservative attitude toward modern living. Or perhaps since the design of his own residence gave him the ideal opportunity to create a presentation for future clients, he may have deliberately tried to reflect the general tastes of the middle-class patrons who supported the architects of the day.

However, in contrast to the house's overall unassuming appearance, when we stop to look at details, such as the lattice-work in the windows and door, we see that the curves distinctive to Art Nouveau are everywhere (photos 47-54). The white ironwork climbing the stone wall like ivy suspends the large balcony (photo 49). Extending up to a height of three stories, this wrought iron seems to represent the growth of a plant or some soft candy that has been stretched and wrapped around the stone. The thick opaque glass used for the floor of the balcony, which projects out over the house's entrance, shows the architect's concern that light not be prevented from reaching this entrance (photo 48). This practical approach to design figures in Horta's talent for converting such indispensable details as the vent cover, door chime, and mud scraper (photo 50) into decorative elements. On the exterior of the house, there is not a single decoration that exists solely for itself.

Maison Horta, which shows the unmistakable hallmark of Art Nouveau in its details, is both house and studio, side by side (photo 45). The left-hand side, number twenty-five, was Horta's private home. Horta made the residential portion of the lot slightly wider, at 20 feet, than the studio. With four stories, including the attic, the house is taller than the studio, which is only three stories high. Also, the street side of the studio's second floor is a salon for the residential house. These decisions demonstrate Horta's desire to give personal living space priority over work space. Horta once said that he approached the design of the studio with the same simplicity with which one would approach the design of a monastery.

On the broad front door of the residence is a bronze handle that clings to the door like an inchworm (photo 53). When we push open the door, an inner door—a double-leafed hinged door inlaid with stained glass—appears (photo 56). Here the subdued quality of the exterior undergoes a complete transformation, and we enter, at last, into the exuberant world of Art Nouveau.

A World of Exuberant Sensuality

When we step inside the entrance hall, we encounter a space filled with the radiance of Carrara marble, which covers the floor, stairways, and walls (photos 55-59). The brass radiator gleams quietly with a golden sheen. Turning back, we see the stained glass of the inner doors drawing in light from the street and displaying mysterious flowers (photo 55). The first floor of the house consists of this entrance hall plus service rooms such as the kitchen and laundry room arranged in back of it.

The single, heavy handrail of oak rises from a marble pedestal alongside the stairs (photo 57). Our eyes instinctively follow the handrail as it extends up the spiral staircase and invites us to the fourth floor in a single breath. Looking up from below, we can see that this stairwell, which vertically pierces the interior of the house, is topped with a stained glass skylight. The sun that streams down through the skylight transforms the stairwell into a tube of light. This light, along with the curve of the handrail, becomes the sign that leads us effortlessly into the interior.

First, let us follow the invitation of the light to the fourth floor (photos 70-78). The stained glass of the skylight forms a large floral design. On the brown wall directly below, a mirror image of these flowers is outlined in gold. Since the light

fixtures and brass ornamentation also use a floral motif, twisting around the pillars that support the skylight, we get the impression that we have wandered into a man-made flower garden (photos 71 & 75). The facing mirrors affixed to the walls reflect each other, giving us a sense of unending space in this narrow landing (photo 74). The stairwell, in fact, is the crowning glory of this home's interior. Amazingly enough, the staircase is a hanging structure, supported by the columns from the skylight. However, this innovative structural form is completely undetectable.

The interior structure of the house divides the floors according to function. On the first floor is the entrance hall and utility space; on the second floor, a public space comprised of dining room, smoking room, and salon; and on the third and fourth floors, Horta's private living space. In other words, the function of each room is assigned vertically, with the stairwell central to the structure. A small service staircase hidden behind the stairwell makes it possible for all domestic chores to be carried out without being seen by master or guest.

Differences in the personalities of each floor are reflected naturally in their interior designs. The second floor is furnished in a manner suitable for receiving guests, and richly lustrous materials — marble and colored tiles — were selected for the walls. The door handles, each of which has a unique design, exemplify Horta's profound attention to detail. The dining room and salon are essentially open spaces, and it is easy to picture guests relaxing here. The third floor, on the other hand, is extremely simple (photos 79-90), with white plaster walls in the bedroom and a moss green willow leaf wallpaper designed by William Morris in the study. The various rooms are divided by

Layout of second floor

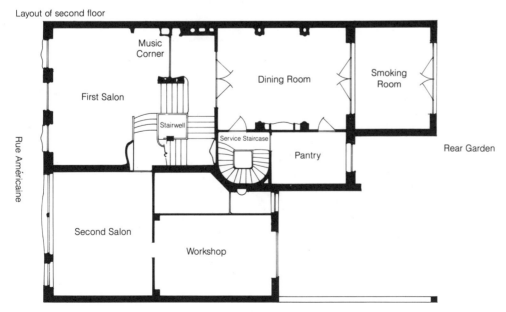

doors, eloquently expressing Horta's concern for protecting privacy within the living space. The wallpaper with its subdued color (photo 81) is particularly comforting.

Along with the stairwell, the interior of the second floor with its open, public spaces is another highlight of this house (photos 60 & 61). As we climb the stairs from the entrance hall, the dining room with its barrel vault stretches out on our right. Beyond this lie the smoking room and rear garden. The smoking room was added in order to change the atmosphere of the house (photo 104) when Horta remarried in 1906. On the left, a few steps higher, are the music room, and further in, a salon that extends into the studio portion of the house (photo 103). The dining room and salon are not connected in a straight line: the central point is shifted subtly. The heights of the floors also differ, so that although the whole space is open, it is divided into two separate rooms. In European high society at the end of the nineteenth century, it was considered common sense to establish two different spaces for guests: one for dining, the other for conversing and talking business.

In the interior of the dining room, numerous classic examples of Art Nouveau design catch our eyes (photos 92-101). The white tile that brightens the ceiling (photo 95) was originally intended for the exterior wall facing the garden. The skirting of the walls is decorated with beautiful stripes of marble, and the periphery of the floor is embellished with a marble mosaic in the form of swaying water plants (photo 101). The center of the floor, done in parquet, was probably intended to prevent scratches to the furniture. Set into the wall below the fixed display shelf is a gas stove (photos 97 & 100). This too seems to have been designed by Horta himself, and its sheet copper border

and stopcock express a certain voluptuousness. Horta's attention extended not only to the furniture but also to all details, even door hinges and keyholes.

Every detail of architecture becomes ornamentation. Few works make this Art Nouveau characteristic more clearly visual than Maison Horta. And yet, there is not one decoration that is meaningless. The swaying water plants on the floor of the dining room, the doorknob shaped like a twisting vine (photo 94), and the lamps that curl around the supporting columns—the sensual curves drawn by such details all seem to work in unison with the larger flow of space beginning at the stairwell. That single handrail rising from the heavy pedestal in the entrance hall starts the flow. Its endlessly curving line draws the visitor effortlessly into the interior of the house. This movement reveals the essential Horta, an architect who never became trapped by ornamentation.

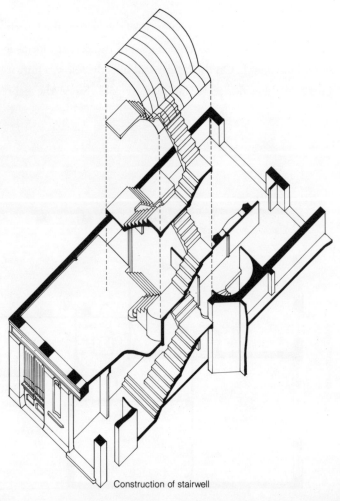

Construction of stairwell

104

Chapter 3

HILL HOUSE

1 9 0 3 – 1 9 0 4

Charles Rennie Mackintosh

Helensburgh, Scotland

105

105
Walking to the front door on the west
side of the house, the visitor looks out
at the Clyde Estuary below.

107

106
The sandstone frame of the library window. Today the library is used as a
reception office.

107
The entrance, protected by thick sandstone, looks something like a small
cave.

108 An overall view from the southwest. The precisely crafted rainproof plaster walls are peculiar to this region.

109
Chimney, dressing room eaves, and roof
create a geometric composition on the
upper part of the western wall.

110
A view from the lawn shows a picturesque beauty reminiscent of an old
castle.

111
The bay window also serves as a sun-
room and can be entered from the
garden.

112
The library window facing the garden.
The bulge of the second floor bedroom
window above forms the eaves.

114

113
The entrance hall. The grid-patterned
carpet differs from the original carpet.

114
Inside the entrance hall, the latticework
front door is on the left, the stairs on
the right.

115
A simply designed fireplace in the entrance hall just in front of the steps.

116

116
The ceiling lamps, made of glass set in metal frames, look like Japanese paper-covered lamp stands.

117
A pine clock and an oak chair based on the grid pattern in the inner part of the entrance hall.

118

118
The first floor living room door with a
tasteful purple grid. The knob is an egg-
shaped handle.

119
The glass in the bay window is not
plate glass but small rectangles set into
a lead grid.

122

120
The bay window of the living room with
oak armchairs on either side is bathed
in full sunlight.

121
A stylized rose is carved out of the top
of each post.

122
The latticework table with grids of inlaid
shell in the center was added in 1908.

123

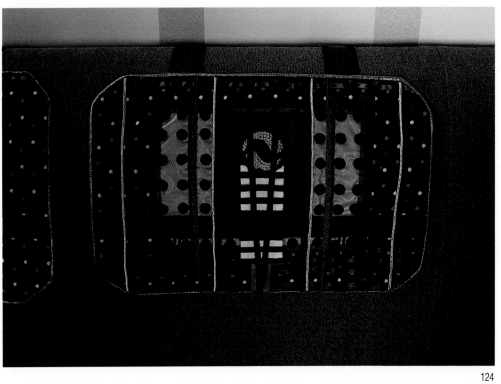

124

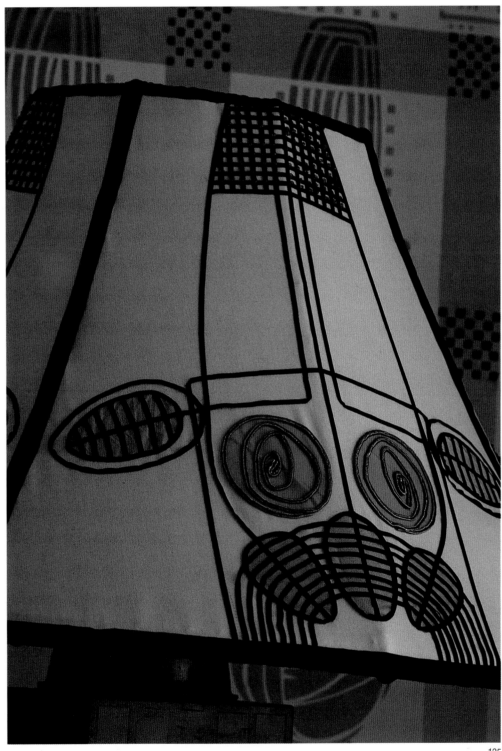

125

123
The piano corner of the living room. In
the foreground is a mahogany couch.

124
Rose patterns have been appliqued onto
the heavy upholstery of the couch.

125
The embroidered shade on the living
room floor lamp was added in later years.

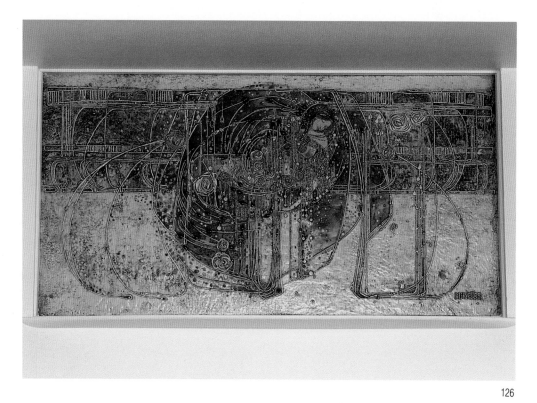

126
The plaster of paris relief above the living room fireplace is the work of Mackintosh's wife, Margaret.

127
Curved pine makes the hearth an alcove, with display shelves on each side.

128

129

128
The decorations on the fireplace, composed of cloisonné and mirror, are the
most elaborate details in the house.

129
Roses and a vertical lattice with grid
pattern are stenciled on the walls
around the living room.

130

131

130
A stained glass side lamp attached to the upper part of the wall in the living room.

131
The lamp above the dining table in the first floor dining room is reminiscent of a large Japanese lamp.

132
The side lamp in the dining room looks exactly like a Japanese paper-covered lamp stand turned upside down.

133

133
The dining room fireplace with a steel
plate around the opening. Grids of fireproof tile decorate the wall.

134
The landing of the staircase, decorated
with a chair. The lamp is made of
chromium-plated iron.

138

139

135
A post, set with colored glass, separates the entrance hall and the stairwell.

136
The north wall of the stairwell curves outward. The thin post is slightly convex, forming an entasis.

137
The design of the lamp that hangs from wires in the stairwell is also based on a grid pattern.

138
The original carpet was designed with scattered, isolated grid patterns.

139
A rug in the dressing room.

140
The dressing room, which gets its light from the window above the front door, and a chest with mirror.

141
The shower in the bathroom of the second
floor guest room is also Mackintosh's
design.

142
The fireplace in the second floor guest
room. Each room's fireplace has its own
unique design.

143
The fireplace in the master bedroom is made of steel and white pine with a shelf built above it.

144
A side lamp in the master bedroom made of brass and frosted glass.

145
Geometric patterns of colored glass and mirror set into the steel of the fireplace.

144

145

147

148

146
Of all the interior design, the area around the hearth of the master bedroom was given the most attention.

147
The bedroom's full-length mirror, with a tray on either side, was also inlaid with colored glass grids.

148, 149
Geometric lead patterns and small hanging knobs add color to the bedroom washstand.

149

◀ 150 Along the east wall of the bedroom are built-in wardrobes and a chair, which is essentially an objet d'art.

151 The vault ceiling curves up gently over the bed, which has no headboard.

152

152
A window overlooking the garden is set
into an alcove in the bedroom.

Mackintosh, Interior Designer

Charles Rennie Mackintosh was born in Glasgow in 1868, the son of a policeman and the second of eleven children. His was certainly not a well-to-do family, and because of this, he never received a formal higher education in architecture. Since Mackintosh had demonstrated a talent for design at an early age, he began a five-year apprenticeship at a local design firm in 1884 when he turned sixteen. At the same time, he attended night classes at the Glasgow School of Art, which he later redesigned into one of his most renowned and individual works. Mackintosh was educated in the architectural style then current in late Victorian Great Britain, which showed the influence of John Ruskin in its orientation toward medievalism and a return to nature.

On finishing his apprenticeship in 1889, Mackintosh began work as a draftsman for the Honeyman and Keppie design firm. He realized most of his major achievements as a member of this firm over the next twenty-four years. In 1891, he made his first trip to Italy and spent time in city after city observing Renaissance architecture. During this period he also began to participate actively in competitions and won several awards.

The delicate aestheticism that came to characterize Mackintosh's design was profoundly related to the Arts and Crafts design movement of a group known as "The Four," which included his wife. The designs of this group of four from Glasgow were more appreciated on the European continent than in Great Britain. The extraordinary response their work received at the eighth Vienna *Secession* exhibition in 1900 is a case in point. In fact, Mackintosh's style, with its strong tendency toward color interiors with rectilinear decoration, resembled that of Josef Hoffman's Viennese workshop. As Mackintosh began to distinguish himself in his field, he seriously expanded the scope of his design activities at the very end of the century.

In 1896, he won a competition for the design that was to become the crowning achievement of his career: the redesign of the Glasgow School of Art. In its construction, completed in two stages, he set forth a modernity that calls to mind American skyscraper architecture along with a reinterpretation of traditional Scottish architectural forms. At the same time, he turned his hand to the design of countless interior items such as furniture, attaching great importance to the unity of all aspects of an interior. He was, in a sense, the first modern interior designer. The furniture designs he turned out during his life number more than three hundred. These designs were used characteristically in such shops as the Willow Tearooms (1904), commissioned by Miss Cranston, his patron from 1900 on. Mackintosh also provided two residences in the suburbs of Glasgow, Windy Hill (1901) and Hill House (1903-1904), with as much original furniture as the clients allowed.

Around 1910, Mackintosh's activities suddenly began to decline. He resigned his position at the Honeyman and Keppie firm in 1913, and the following year he left Glasgow. According to one theory, the fact that he was so respected in Germany turned out to be a curse: he lost one job after another, as if in response to the outbreak of World War I. His later years are said to have been dark, his days plagued by alcoholism and emotional instability. He only painted an occasional watercolor of the landscapes and flowers he loved. It was as if his life were the physical manifestation of Art Nouveau's rise and fall. In 1928,

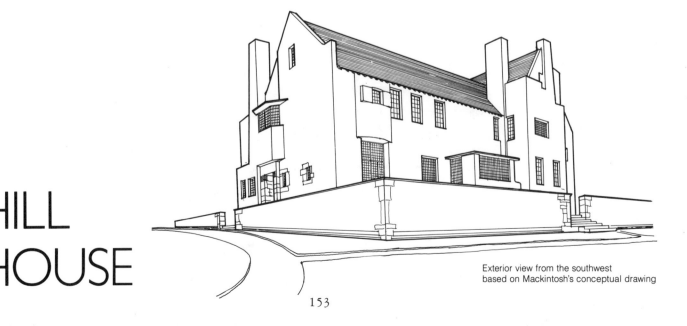

HILL
HOUSE

Exterior view from the southwest
based on Mackintosh's conceptual drawing

Mackintosh passed away in London, far from his hometown, the victim of tongue cancer.

The View of Hill House

Helensburgh today is a short hour's train ride from Glasgow's Queens Street station. This small town seems to have been a suburban district newly developed in the late nineteenth century when Glasgow's heavy industries were thriving. Hill House is about half an hour's walk from the Helensburgh station. Along the road to Hill House we can see grand, somewhat aged residences that appear to be the homes of the wealthy in days gone by. A common dream in Victorian Great Britain, as implied in the 1860s song "Home Sweet Home," was to set up a home of one's own in the suburbs. Walter W. Blackie, the man who commissioned Hill House, was himself a businessman and made his fortune in publishing.

Hill House today is the property of the National Trust, a private voluntary group in Great Britain, and is preserved and open to the public. Because of this, few furnishings have been lost or altered and the essence of Mackintosh's interior design remains for everyone to experience. The fact that you can also glimpse the life-style of the middle class at the beginning of the twentieth century makes a visit here worthwhile.

As the name suggests, Hill House is built on a small hill. It has a broad site overlooking the Clyde Estuary, which has sustained Glasgow's industry. From the path between the gate and the front door, you can faintly see the estuary beyond the lawn and the rose garden to the south (photo 105).

The exterior of the house is finished with a plaster that resembles gray mortar. Such exteriors are traditional in rainy Scotland. The slate roof on top of the house gives its front a rather stark appearance (photos 105-109). To many like myself the effect must seem unexpectedly far removed from the sumptuousness of Art Nouveau. Only the dash of white in the window sashes and the little eaves that quietly cap the second floor bay window hint at Mackintosh's design.

We should, before entering, take a walk around the garden, and from there look up at the house, built on a base raised one level above the garden (photo 108). Seen from this vantage point, Hill House looks quite picturesque (photos 110-112), especially in contrast with its blunt, somewhat forbidding front. A forest of chimneys reaches up from the house, the number originating from the many fireplaces inside. Among them towers the cylindrical shape of the service staircase. The conical roof of the staircase is exactly like that of the old castles that can be seen here and there throughout Scotland. Directly below is a bower that looks like a guardhouse, and the roofs of both act together magnificently to reinforce the image of a castle. The garden was undoubtedly the site of many parties, for which Hill House's lovely exterior is an ideal setting.

What was foremost in Blackie's mind when he commissioned the design was not the entertainment of guests, but rather, spending pleasant weekends together with his family. This was the whole point of a suburban home. Hill House's character can be said to differ essentially from urban homes such as the Casa Batlló or Maison Horta. Before beginning his design, Mackintosh took every available opportunity to spend time with the Blackie family. This gave him a firm grasp of their living habits. Whether a result of this or not, Mackintosh's plan was accepted with few alterations by the client. Blackie's additions were a

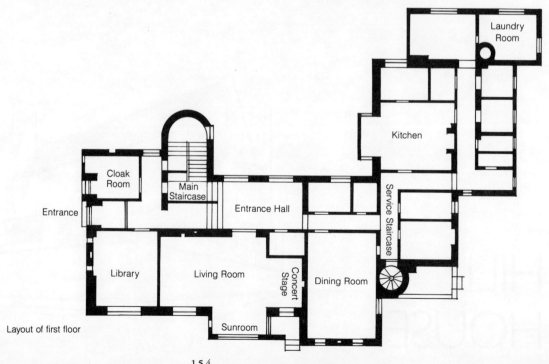

Layout of first floor

154

library and a billiard room—which was never actually built—for entertaining guests. For budgetary reasons, one further condition was that the rooms other than the entrance hall and bedroom would not be provided with much furniture or household effects at first.

The front door is fashioned with a thick latticework design (photo 107). Lattice was a favorite pattern of Mackintosh's and may have been derived from a Japanese style popular among Art Nouveau artists and designers. Opening this door, we find the library on the right. The billiard room was planned to be built on the left. A few steps up, the entrance hall stretches out before us (photos 113-117). A grid pattern in a tasteful shade of purple is woven into the gray foundation of the carpet on the steps. The rectangular parallelepiped of the entrance hall with its vertical strips of brown-painted pine emphasizes a pattern of straight lines (photo 117), and the ceiling lights, looking like upside-down Japanese paper lanterns, are square (photo 116). Only the stenciled purple roses give some curvilinear color to the white walls.

The configuration of this linear interior that takes lattice as its basis sets up a clear distinction between Mackintosh and Gaudí or Horta. The way in which rooms are connected differs, too, with each dividing at right angles into the next rather than having spaces move fluidly, one into the other. Given his design preferences, Mackintosh seemed to be a designer closer to Art Deco than to Art Nouveau.

Variation in the movement of interior space is not meager, however. As we step out of the sober, calm atmosphere of the entrance hall, we experience a complete change of mood upon entering the neat, pure-white living room (photos 118-130).

Directly across from the living room entrance, a soft light shines through the bay windows, which face south and enclose an area that serves as a sun-room (photo 120). To our left is a piano corner (photo 123), where the Blackie children apparently put on a home concert every now and then. The area around the fireplace, which occupies half the living room, is decorated by a grid-patterned rug and arranged with warm-colored furniture, which changes the effect further. The finish of the fireplace reveals the designer's extreme meticulousness, with cloisonné work inlaid with fragments of mirror floating against a mosaic background of fireproof tiles (photos 127 & 128). And, as if to emphasize the warmth of the hearth, Mackintosh hollowed out the wall to create a slight alcove.

In a single living room, Mackintosh delineated three separate areas, each with a different face: the sun-room for the afternoon, the hearth for evenings or wintertime family gatherings, and the piano corner where he went to the trouble of lowering the ceiling and building a small stage. The overall decorative motif was the rose. Variously stylized roses ornament the fabric of the curtains and sofa, the stenciled patterns on the surrounding walls, the back of the couch, and the shades of the floor lamp and the wall light. The rose was the flower Mackintosh loved most dearly.

Furniture as Objet D'Art

Perpendicular to the entrance hall is a U-shaped stairwell (photos 134-137). On each of the two landings is a chair. These chairs were not used for sitting but for ornamentation. In one of the posts that divide the entrance hall and the stairwell, elliptical holes have been cut out and set with bright purple glass (photo 135). The glass shines from the light of the upstairs window. From this sort of subtle decoration, I sensed a feminine richness in Mackintosh's sensibility: each room seems to have its own makeup, so exquisitely applied as to be unnoticeable.

On the second floor is a private space composed of bath, dressing room, and bedroom. These are connected by a hall on the north side in which sits a box-shaped waiting seat known as an inglenook. The same transformation of atmosphere achieved between the entrance hall and the living room is repeated in the second floor hall and bedroom. The bedroom appears before us, again unexpectedly, in total whiteness. The bedroom, too, is divided into two areas (photos 143-152): the area around the bed, with its low vault that changes the L-shaped plan of the ceiling (photo 151), and the corner for visiting and chatting, with the fireplace as its center (photo 146).

The curved ceiling that gently arches above the bed looks like a modern translation of the canopied beds favored by European royalty. The low ceiling lends intimacy to the space, and the area around the fireplace forms an alcove with a fixed sofa adjacent to the fireplace. At one time, delicate roses drawn on the surrounding white walls of the room called to mind the graceful outlines of young maidens. A bedroom such as this one, which creates an atmosphere of purity and yet has such warmth, is rare indeed. Between two wardrobes is Mackintosh's most famous piece of furniture, a chair of unusual proportions, small, yet with a very high back (photo 150). He designed this chair uniquely for this bedroom. The fact that he specified its exact placement suggests that it is not so much a chair for sitting as an objet d'art for decoration.

More than anything else, the white interiors realized in the living room and bedroom of Hill House sensitively capture the atmosphere of the house's natural setting. When we look at the rectangular layout of the rooms, the highly stylized roses (photos 125 & 129), and the extensive use of lattice patterns, it doesn't seem that Mackintosh intended to represent nature directly. Most of the Art Nouveau artists tried to hold on to nature, to capture it in their designs. Doesn't it seem that Mackintosh, in contrast, thought to bring people's living spaces closer to nature? The variations of sunlight, the changes of seasons, the rustling movements of trees—the white interior of Hill House is a mirror, reflecting nature's every breath.

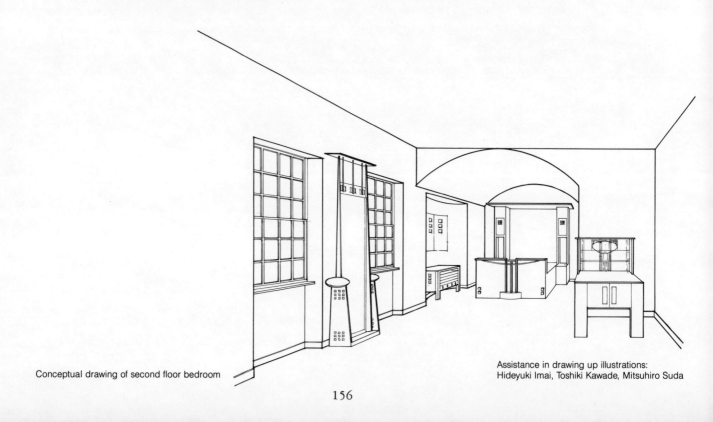

Conceptual drawing of second floor bedroom

Assistance in drawing up illustrations:
Hideyuki Imai, Toshiki Kawade, Mitsuhiro Suda

Chapter 4

ADDITIONAL RESIDENCES
STANDEN
1892 – 1894
Philip Webb
East Grinstead, England

153

153
The south side facing the garden with
the greenhouse on the left. The five-
peaked gable roof houses the living
room and dining room.

154

155

156

157

154
Looking at the living room from the entrance hall. The curtains and carpet are by William Morris.

155
The alcove of the billiard room with its round window surrounded by wallpaper. The window looks out to the greenhouse.

156
A washstand of Victorian design in the dressing room of the second floor bedroom.

157
The stairwell, with its oak handrail and wallpaper, has an air of handmade simplicity.

158
The ceilings of the rooms, beginning with the stairwell, are painted white and create a bright interior.

159
The billiard room, where men would play a game or talk after dinner.

MAISON COHN-DONNAY

1904
Paul Hamesse
Brussels, Belgium

160

160
Looking at the smoking room from the billiard room. The light from outside illuminates the stained glass divider.

161
Pelicans on the cover of the smoking room fireplace, which also serves as a display shelf.

HÔTEL MEZZARA

1910 - 1911
Hector Guimard
Paris, France

162
The entrance to Hôtel Mezzara stands behind an iron fence. The front of the building faces rue Fontaine.

163
A view from the rear garden shows the complex interior structure, with two stories on the left and three stories on the right.

164
A hall in which Mezzara displayed his textile collection to clients.

165
The skylight in the hall ceiling is designed in a symmetrical curving pattern.

164

CASA NAVAS

1901

Lluís Domènech I Montaner

Reus, Spain

166

The dining room and, further back, a
corner by the hearth for chatting. The
lamp was designed by Domènech.

168

169

167
The hall is both waiting room and court-yard in this house. The ceiling was damaged during the Spanish Civil War.

168
The stairwell also serves as an entrance hall. The marble mosaic stairs seem to float to the floor above.

169
The third floor music room. The mosaic fireplace has a peacock-shaped screen.

170
The second floor bathroom, separated from the hall by a single wall of stained glass.

171
A symmetrical mosaic pattern made out of marble chips decorates the floor of the entrance hall.

170

CASA AMATLLER

1898 - 1900
Josep Puig I Cadafalch
Barcelona, Spain

172

172
On the left are the two entrances, one
for people and one for carriages.

173
The skylight in the ceiling of the stairwell. The dot pattern is characteristic of
modernismo designs.

174
The stairwell also serves as a patio. The
somber metalwork of the lamps is eye-
catching.

175
An Islamic-style design peeks down
from the ceiling above a chandelier in
the second floor salon.

174

MAJOLIKAHAUS

1898 – 1899

Otto Wagner

Vienna, Austria

177

176
Gold-colored plaster medallions decorate the wall of the apartment adjacent to Majolikahaus.

177
Two apartments of contrasting designs are separated by a terrace.

178
Art Deco lettering marks the entrance facing a back street.

GROSSES HAUS GLÜCKERT

1901

Joseph Maria Olbrich

Darmstadt, Germany

179

179
An exterior view from the lawn shows
the gabled roof that hangs down like
hair. Flowers are carved into its edges.

180

181

182

183

180
The front, with its semicircular entrance.
The rain gutters jut out from either side
in the shape of birds.

181, 182
From the staircase and the entrance
hall, the designer's austere treatment of
detail can be seen.

183
The fireplace in the main wall of the entrance hall is decorated with Byzantine-
style ornamentation.

A Blossoming New Art

The more or less twenty-year period from around 1890 to 1910 was an age in which Art Nouveau architecture, as if caught up in a feverish delirium, bloomed in many different colors and forms throughout the cities of Europe. Soon after the First World War, however, the life of this art movement, which took the beauty of natural forms such as flowers for its motifs, withered rapidly. In this way, Art Nouveau itself can be thought of as a flower.

Art Nouveau was known by a variety of names in different tongues and among different peoples: it was called *Jugendstil* in Germany, *Secession* in Austria, *modernismo* in Spain, and *Stile Liberty* in Italy. All of these forms, as the French term Art Nouveau, or New Art, indicates, signified a parting with traditional styles and a search for an architectural space more suitable to the new age that was the twentieth century.

Although the flower was a common motif, each region had its own style of interpretation, such as *modernismo*'s profound ties with Catalan traditions. Let us now look at some of the representative houses that survive in Europe. In the breadth of their expression we can detect the beginnings of the succeeding decorative styles of Modernism and Art Deco.

Simplicity and Warmth: Standen House

Many see the source of Art Nouveau as the Arts and Crafts movement that developed around William Morris, a late-nineteenth-century English thinker and artist. In fact, the floral wallpaper that Morris and Co. began to manufacture on a large scale in the 1870s was popular not only in England but also was exported throughout Europe and revolutionized interior design.

A close friend of Morris, architect Philip Webb (1831-1915), built Standen House in 1894 in a London suburb. The spirit of the Arts and Crafts movement breathes through every nook and cranny of this house. The client James Bell was a successful Birmingham lawyer. When setting up an office in London, he had Standen House built so that he could enjoy his farms on the weekends. This country house with a garden and three farms occupies one of the gently sloping hills found throughout England. There are twelve bedrooms, including the guest rooms. Throughout the interior the rooms are either painted white or decorated with pale wallpaper by Morris and Co. This may be a reflection of the times; electric lighting had gradually become popular, and there was a demand for a healthy brightness in interiors.

In the billiard room, which was a standard in late Victorian homes; the greenhouse, which also served as a living room; and the morning room, used by the lady of the house for reading or for her hobbies, the interior design conveys a handmade warmth through its use of wallpaper, fireplaces, lamps, and other furnishings. The interior has an air of simplicity, rather than the cosmopolitan sophistication of Art Nouveau, and was both for the enjoyment of quiet country living and an expression of the medievalism that was central to the ideology of the Arts and Crafts movement. This concept of design was unique to England.

A Foreshadowing of Art Deco: Maison Cohn-Donnay

In Brussels, shortly before the end of the century, Art

ADDITIONAL RESIDENCES

Nouveau design as initiated by Victor Horta became a sensation. A great many young architects and interior designers created an abundance of variations in their styles. Unlike Maison Horta, the design of Maison Cohn-Donnay, whose interior was renovated in 1904 by the young artist Paul Hamesse (1877-1956), is dominated by a linear and graphic style of decoration. Upon entering the entrance hall, we see a billiard room and smoking room stretching toward the courtyard in a single sweep. In the glass door separating the two rooms, stained glass set in flowing curves lends gaiety to the interior. On both of the two heaters are brass covers emblazoned with pelicans. The rooms are not joined by fluid curves. In this way, Hamesse is closer to Mackintosh and may be best described as an artist whose work presages Art Deco.

Graceful Curves: Hôtel Mezzara

In talking about Art Nouveau, of course, Paris can't be overlooked. This city saw the rise of Emile Gallé, Louis Majorelle, and countless other craftsmen and designers of interior furnishings. Central among the architects was Hector Guimard (1867-1942), known for Castel Beranger (1898), the apartment house that was Paris's first Art Nouveau building, and the entrances to the métro (1905). Paris was the mecca of the movement, yet, sadly, very few houses remain that retain their original interiors. In fashion-conscious Paris, these interiors must have undergone one change after another as Modernism and Art Deco flourished.

Hôtel Mezzara in the sixteenth arrondissement was built late in Guimard's career in 1911. Presently it is used as a girls' dormitory, and except for the main structure of the building,

most of the interior has, unsurprisingly, been lost. In this design Guimard does not show the same concern for detail he once did. The iron fence that faces rue Fontaine is so attenuated it cannot be compared with the métro entrances. As with Horta, however, curved ornamentation still creates a graceful flow in the interior design. This fluidity clearly distinguishes Guimard as a principal artist of Art Nouveau. In the stairwell, where a guitar-shaped skylight filters light down to the first floor, the staircase supported by a steel frame and the upstairs gallery present a magnificent and graceful line. We can say, until the end, Guimard never once forgot that ornament takes meaning only from the context of its space.

Ornament to Dazzle the Eye: Casa Navas

One aspect of the *modernismo* movement of Catalonia that clearly differed from Art Nouveau in general was its strong link to the independent spirit of the people of the region. Any trace of the influence of Japanese plastic arts usually prevalent in Art Nouveau is difficult to find. Instead, the Spanish explored their own roots, taking the study of the architectural styles fostered by the history and religious faith of the people as major themes. In 1888, Barcelona's World's Fair became the occasion for the appearance of *modernismo* as a new style for the creation of urban spaces. Lluís Domènech i Montaner (1850-1923), Josep Puig i Cadafalch (1869-1956), and Antonio Gaudí were the central figures of the movement.

Domènech, who was of the same generation as Gaudí, was more politically active and his style bears the strong mark of Catalanism. Casa Navas, which stands in the center of Gaudí's hometown of Reus, was built in 1901 in the middle years of

Domènech's career. The house belonged to textile maker Joan Navas, and its first floor is occupied by a shop. Its motif is the rose, a flower much loved in the region.

There is certainly no one whose eyes would not be dazzled by the abundance of ornamentation in the stairwell, which also serves as the entrance hall. With its mosaic floor and plaster relief on the ceiling and walls, the room seems consumed by the designer's zeal not to leave a single blank surface anywhere. In addition, the upstairs hall is filled with stone carvings and stained glass, and we feel as if we were choking in the hot air of a profusion of blooming flowers. In the dining room, music room, or any other room, we see spread out before us an opulent display of ornamentation to rival anything in Paris or Brussels. Finally, even the bathroom is enclosed in stained glass and ornamental tile, and Gaudí's forms begin to seem plain by comparison. The descendants of the Navas family live here to this day, preserving the original interior.

A Hint of Tradition: Casa Amatller

Puig, a generation younger than Domènech and Gaudí, was something of a scholarly architect. He was versed in Latin and was known as a student of medieval architecture. His designs, based on a rich body of knowledge, were strongly inclined toward a rational eclecticism.

Casa Amatller, finished in 1900, is representative of his work and stands adjacent to Casa Batlló. Built earlier as part of the city's expansion plan, the house was redesigned by Puig for the only daughter of the Amatller family. Like Gaudí's Casa Batlló, the design theme is said to be the battle between Saint George and the dragon. On the wall above one of the entrances, wi-

dened to allow carriages to pass, are images of beautiful young girls. Nothing else about the exterior directly brings Art Nouveau to mind, and the wall decorations seem almost Islamic in design. Dragons' faces are set into the ironwork of the balcony. On entering, we see the stairwell, which also acts as a patio, and a skylight in the ceiling inlaid with flowers and dots. The design of this hall, which actively brings in outside light as seen in Casa Navas, is redolent of traditional Spanish patio design, an integral part of older Spanish buildings. Such considerations vary from the concept behind Casa Batlló and are a part of Puig's sense of historicism.

Gorgeous Tile Decor: Majolikahaus

In Vienna, the capital of the Austro-Hungarian Empire, Otto Wagner (1841-1918), the city architect, worked on a great many public buildings starting from the end of the century, and it was he who brought Art Nouveau to Vienna at the movement's outset. Vienna, like Paris and Barcelona, was undergoing urban reorganization.

Majolikahaus, an apartment building built in 1899 concurrent with the consolidation of a new loop road, became one of Wagner's representative works. Just as the name implies, its entire exterior wall is covered with brilliant floral-motif Majolican tile. The flower patterns of the tiles stand out slightly, like a relief, and wonderfully express the freshness of live flowers. These tiles were not used merely for decoration; in order to protect buildings from the coke soot that polluted the air, Wagner advocated finishing the surfaces of buildings with tile as often as opportunity allowed. The walls of the neighboring apartment building, which was constructed at the same time, are decorated with gold plaster medallions portraying women's faces and peacocks. The extreme grandeur of the design seems to express a nostalgic yearning for the gaiety of Viennese Baroque.

Geometric Composition: Grosses Haus Glückert

As magnate of the Viennese architecture world, Wagner had a great many followers. One of his leading disciples, Joseph Maria Olbrich (1867-1908), was one of the central figures in the *Secession* movement. At the invitation of Ludwig IV, the Grand Duke of Hesse, he moved to Darmstadt in Germany to work on the construction of an artists' colony on Mathildenhohe hill. Looking at one house from this group of works, Grosses Haus Glückert, built in 1901, we can easily comprehend Olbrich's eccentric style of expression.

The roof hangs down large and full like a woman's bobbed haircut. The entrance looks like a gaping mouth. We can well imagine that he was personifying the house. Though flowers are cut into the corners of the walls in sharp relief, they don't cover the whole wall. A heavy fireplace is set into the facing wall of the interior hall. In the peacock pattern that stretches up behind the fireplace, such details as the tone of the colors lend an exotic air reminiscent of Byzantine art. As we can see from the shape of the fireplace, the handrail of the staircase, or the lamps, Olbrich did not refine his detailing excessively. What he did instead was find interest in the composition of geometric forms. This sensibility, which foreshadowed Art Deco, seems related to Mackintosh, who was highly regarded in Germany.

From Nouveau to Deco

Strictly speaking, Victor Horta and Hector Guimard can be said to be the two central figures in Art Nouveau. The curves they drew in their handrails or stained glass created a fluid line in space, stretching outward and intertwining. Mackintosh captured the transience of flowers with his graphic style. Gaudí and Domènech traced history in their explorations of their ethnic identity. And Wagner and Olbrich presaged another decorative art form that was soon to appear—Art Deco.

In any case, no European architectural style seems to have ever shown so strong an interest in nature. As Europe became industrialized on a large scale, it felt the urgent need for an expansion and reorganization of its cities in response to the sudden increase in population. The architects of the time were forced to destroy the tranquil, beautiful nature once surrounding these cities. To preserve nature, at least in form—wasn't this the fervent desire of the architects who brought the resplendent flower of Art Nouveau to bloom?